EXTREME WEATHER

Written By: Anna DiGilio

All rights reserved. No part of this publication may be reproduced, distributed, or transmitted in any form or by any means, including photocopying, recording, or other electronic or mechanical methods, without the prior written permission of the publisher, except in the case of brief quotations embodied in critical reviews and certain other noncommercial uses permitted by copyright law.

For permission requests, write to the publisher:
Laprea Publishing
info@lapreapublishing.com

Website: www.GuidedReaders.com

ISBN: 978-1-64579-053-2

© 2017 Anna DiGilio
www.SimplySkilledTeaching.com

Printed in the United States of America

TABLE OF CONTENTS

About the Atmosphere .... Page 4

What Is Weather? .... Page 5

What Is Extreme Weather? .... Page 6

What Are Heat and Cold Waves? .... Page 7

What Are Droughts and Floods? .... Page 8

What Are Hurricanes? .... Page 10

What Are Monsoons? .... Page 12

What Are Tornadoes? .... Page 13

What Are Blizzards? .... Page 14

What the Experts Think .... Page 15

Glossary .... Page 16

About the Atmosphere

Weather occurs in the atmosphere. The atmosphere is a layer of gases. It is invisible. It is all around the earth. The atmosphere is mostly nitrogen and oxygen. There are other gases, too. We breathe this air.

What Is Weather?

Weather is all around you. Your senses tell the weather. You feel the heat and cold outside. You see clouds. You hear thunder. Snow feels cold when you touch it. Weather is rain, wind, snow, and more.

People adjust to weather. In the cold, they wear coats. In the heat, they wear shorts.

Meteorologists study weather. They collect data about a region for a period of time. This tells the climate.

What Is Extreme Weather?

Extreme weather is a surprise where it happens. It cannot always be predicted. There are many extreme weather events like snow, floods, or rain.

Extreme weather harms people and animals. It can cost millions of dollars in damage.

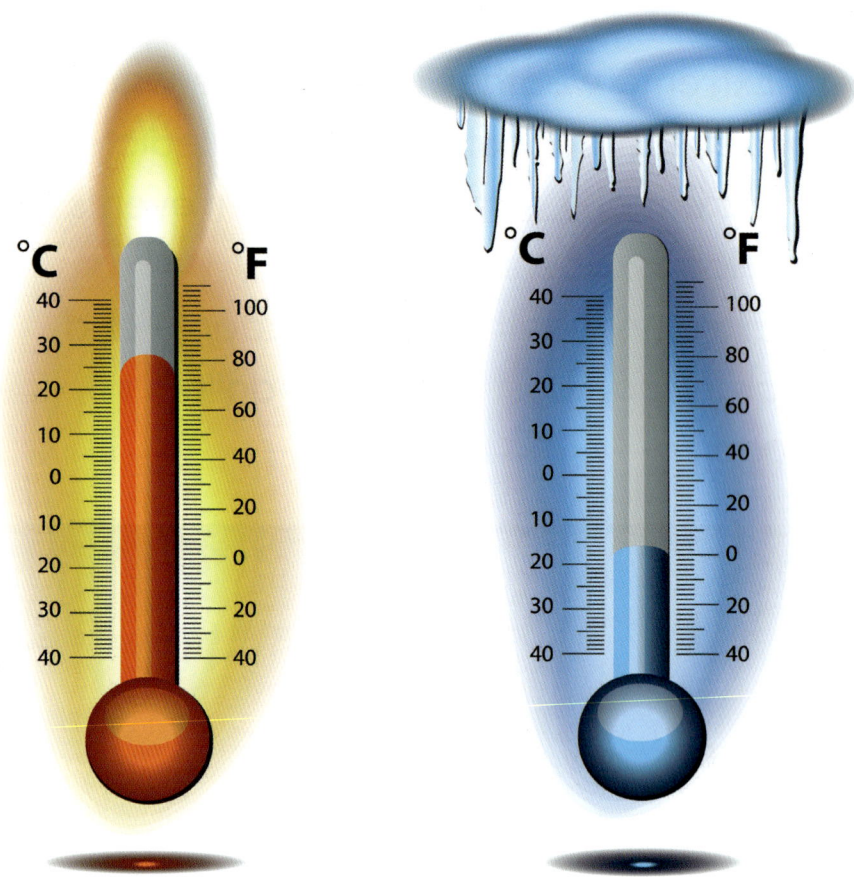

What Are Heat and Cold Waves?

Hot and cold weather can be extreme and can harm people and animals. Long periods of high temperatures are heat waves. Long periods of freezing temperatures are cold waves.

What Are Droughts and Floods?

All living things need fresh water. Many people live near freshwater rivers, lakes, and streams. Weather affects the water cycle. It brings rain and moisture around the world.

Extreme weather can interrupt the water cycle. It can cause droughts. Water sources dry up. Food will not grow. A drought harms living things.

Here is a photograph of polluted water and cracked soil of a dried-out lake during a drought.

Flooding is extreme weather, too. A flood often happens when there is heavy rainfall. Floods cause water to rise higher than the river banks. It fills streets. It destroys homes and injures people. A flood will destroy everything in its path.

What Are Hurricanes?

"Hurricanes" are powerful windstorms. They start above the ocean. When ocean water is warm, it turns into <u>vapor</u>. The vapor rises into the cool air above. A thunderstorm develops and grows. This creates a hurricane.

Some hurricanes get stronger. If they reach land, they can harm property and living things.

The center of the hurricane is called the "eye." It is calm and sunny there. Hurricanes only occur in a small area of the earth. A hurricane in the Pacific Ocean is called a <u>typhoon</u>.

This is a satellite photo of Hurricane Katrina.

What Are Monsoons?

Monsoons are high winds. They occur in Asia. They can bring heavy rains. This is known as a wet monsoon. Monsoons can bring dry, or <u>arid</u>, weather. This is known as a dry monsoon.

This is the aftermath of a monsoon in India.

What Are Tornadoes?

Tornadoes are another type of extreme weather. They are caused by fast-moving air in thunderstorms. The wind might spin as fast as 200 miles an hour.

Tornadoes are very harmful. Today there are early warning detection systems. These devices save lives.

What Are Blizzards?

Blizzards are strong snowstorms that have heavy snow and high winds. Blizzards occur when the air near the earth's surface is very cold. The atmosphere is <u>frigid</u> and filled with moisture.

Sleet, snow, and ice are other forms of winter <u>precipitation</u>, or water falling from the sky.

What the Experts Think

Weather experts think climate change is causing extreme weather. Today's scientists are looking for ways to prevent extreme weather.

You could be a weather expert when you grow up. Extreme weather problem solvers will make tools to stop extreme weather in the future.

GLOSSARY

<u>arid</u>
very dry

<u>frigid</u>
very cold temperature

<u>precipitation</u>
a deposit on the earth of hail, mist, rain, sleet, or snow

<u>typhoon</u>
a violent tropical storm or cyclone in the China Sea and the western Pacific Ocean

<u>vapor</u>
a visible exhalation as fog, mist, steam, smoke, or noxious gas suspended in the air